NOW THE DAY IS OVER

MOREHOUSE PUBLISHING

Morehouse Publishing
P.O. Box 1321
Harrisburg, PA 17105

Morehouse Publishing is a division of The Morehouse Group.

Text: Sabine Baring-Gould (1834-1924)
Music: Merrial, Joseph Barnby (1838-1896)

Printed in China

Cover and page design by Jim Booth.

Library of Congress Cataloging-in-Publication Data

Baring-Gould, S. (Sabine), 1834-1924
    Now the day is over : toddler prayers / words by Sabine Baring-Gould ; illustrated by Preston McDaniels
      p. cm.
    ISBN 0-8192-1868-5
    1. Bedtime prayers. 2. Children—Prayer-books and devotions—English. 3. Presence of God—Juvenile literature. [1. Bedtime prayers. 2. Prayers. 3. Hymns.] I. McDaniels, Preston, ill. II. Title.

BV283.B43 B37 2001
242'.82—dc21
                                                                              00-051120

01 02 03 04 05 06 07 08 09   10 9 8 7 6 5 4 3 2 1

NOW THE DAY IS OVER

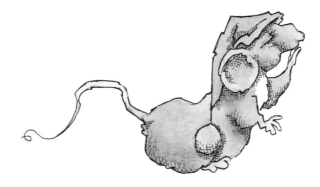

Text by Sabine Baring-Gould

Illustrated by Preston McDaniels

Now the day is over,

Night is drawing nigh,

Shadows of the evening steal across the sky.

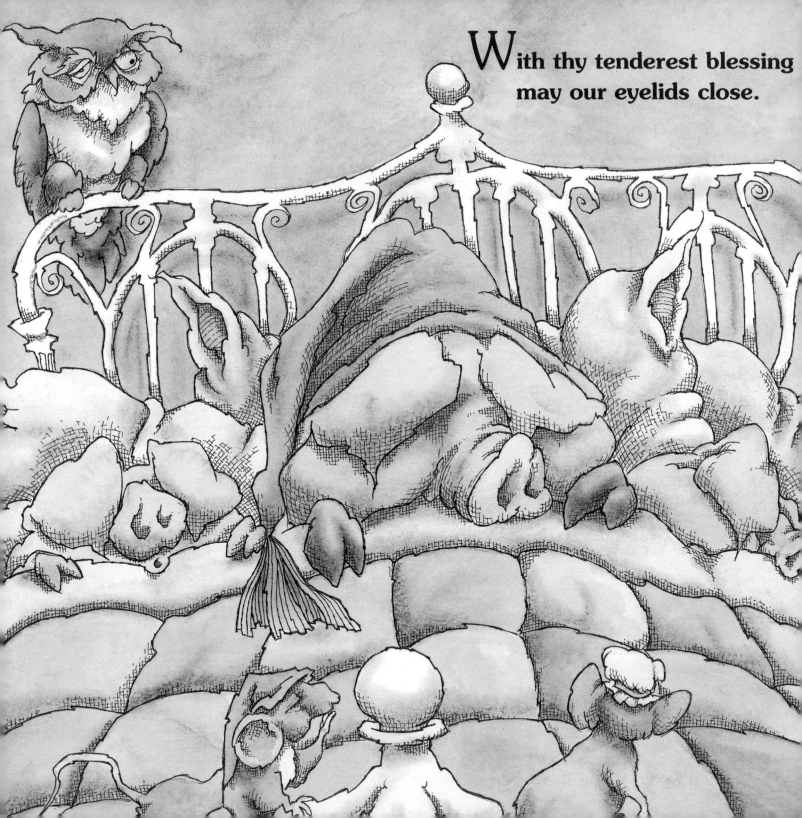

With thy tenderest blessing
may our eyelids close.

Grant the little children visions bright of thee;

Guard the sailors tossing on the deep, blue sea.

Through the long night watches may thine angels spread

their white wings above me,
watching 'round my bed.

When the morning wakens, then may I arise

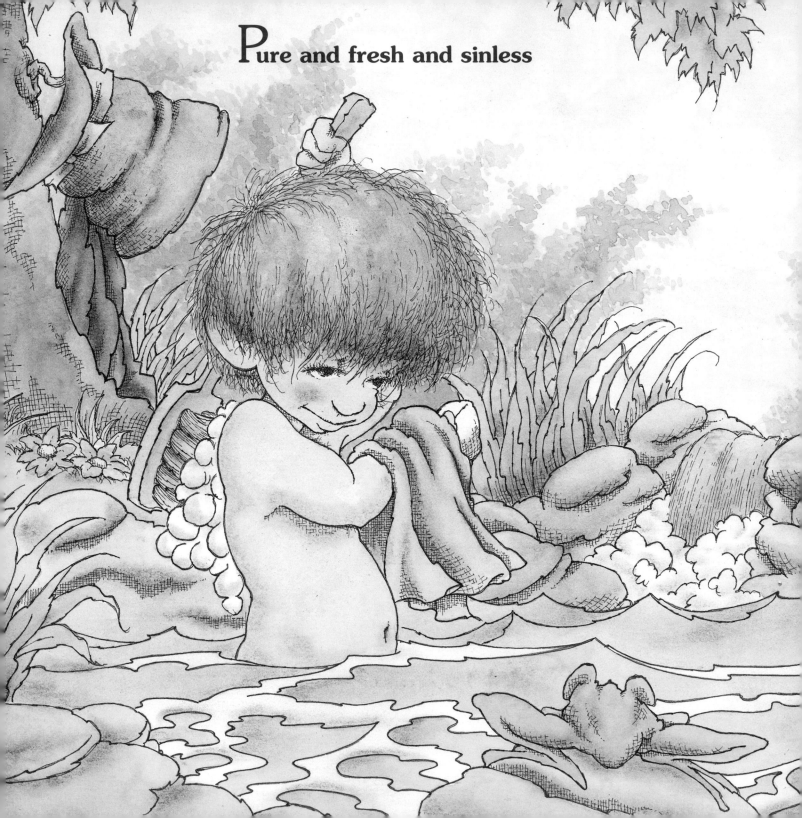

Pure and fresh and sinless

In thy holy eyes.

ALSO ILLUSTRATED BY PRESTON McDANIELS

GOD OF THE SPARROW
hymn by Jaroslav J. Vajda
illustrated by Preston McDaniels

"God of the sparrow
God of the whale
God of the swirling stars
How does the creature say Awe?
How does the creature say Praise?"

In his popular contemporary hymn, "God of the Sparrow," Jaroslav Vajda asks us to observe the wonders of creation all around us and respond to the Creator of it all. How do we, as children of God, express our wonder, love, faith, and sorrow? Preston McDaniels captures these and the remarkable beauty of all that exists—the lovely and the harsh—and helps children (and adults) offer thanks to God. (Ages 3–7)

PRAISE FOR PRESTON McDANIELS' BOOKS

"...LIVELY, COMPELLING ILLUSTRATIONS..." —*CBA MARKETPLACE*
"...CHARMING, LOVELY, REVERENTIAL, JOYFUL..." —*TROY BROADCASTING CORPORATION*
"COLORFUL AND DRAMATIC ILLUSTRATIONS..." —*CATHOLIC PARENT*

ALL THINGS BRIGHT AND BEAUTIFUL
hymn by Cecil Frances Alexander
illustrations by Preston McDaniels

"All things bright and beautiful,
All creatures great and small,
All things wise and wonderful,
The Lord God made them all."

Few hymns portray the joyfulness of creation as beautifully as the classic hymn, "All Things Bright and Beautiful." Its lively tune and colorful images have made it a favorite for many generations. Now Preston McDaniels helps us to appreciate the hymn anew with his energetic and humorous illustrations of all the wonderful things God made. (Ages 3–7)